To: I ♥ you
Love:
Hmeon, 08

My Pen is a Sword

To order additional copies, please contact us.
BookSurge, LLC
www.booksurge.com
1-866-308-6235
orders@booksurge.com

MY PEN IS A SWORD

SWORD

Reflections Of A Conscious Poet

HUTCHIE SIMEON, RAS TAMBA

Pen & Sword Productions
2006

My Pen is a Sword

TABLE OF CONTENTS

ACKNOWLEDGEMENTS

To my son Aidoo, you mean the world to me.

Some of the most important people to me: other family members and close associates who were always there in times of need and those at the Jamaica Daily Gleaner, I will always remember those days.

Lucien Chen, you gave me my first professional writing job, and ever since my pen seems to be always making marks on paper.

Kathy Todd and the Cool Runnings crew, I enjoyed my run with the magazine. That medium helped me to continue writing, giving me an opportunity to publish some of my poems.

My editor M. Douglas Jones, I appreciate your encouragement and continued support.

Soly, Fortunate, Frank and Alpha Blondy, thanks for the hospitality shown to me in Africa. That was my most important mission when my feet touched the Motherland for the first time. Fritzy, I must admit that your contribution was also unique and important as you all made it easier for me being a vegetarian making that journey.

Finally, to all my teachers, from primary school to college, and those members of the community where I grew up who helped to shape my life into who I am today.

FOREWORD

The poems in this selection are a collection of over thirty years of reflections. Some may seem outdated, but at the time they were written, they were prophetic, such as those denouncing apartheid and summoning Nelson Mandela. I humbly give all thanks and praise to JAH that I was able to recite "Welcome, Mandela" upon the occasion of his visit to Jamaica shortly after his release from prison in South Africa.

"Rasta" seeks to express my philosophy of life as an ardent believer in Ras Tafari, while "My Pen is a Sword" defines my purpose as an artist, to defend the underprivileged and oppressed peoples of the world, including the Lost Boys and Girls of Sudan and the people of Haiti.

"State of Emergency" was written about the situation I witnessed in Jamaica during the seventies, but I would also like to extend it now to salute the people of New Orleans who were victimized before, during, or after the hurricanes Katrina and Rita, and all those others around the world who have ever been affected under a state of emergency.

"Foundation" is a call for unity among African peoples in hopes of eliminating the "Chaos" in our Diaspora today. It is my most earnest prayer that leaders and citizens of the world will cease the wanton violence and come together to set better examples for our children.

May those who read these poems find comfort and inspiration, and may JAH bless and guide all.

Hutchie Simeon, Ras Tamba

PEN

MY PEN IS A SWORD

No retreat, no surrender
My pen is a sword
Takes no prisoner
Will not be silenced
Preaches no violence
Voice of the oppressed
Signaling distress
Fighting for humanity
To eradicate poverty
Promoting charity
Exposing authority
My pen is a sword.

Militant and aggressive
Active and assertive
Inciting injunction
Against corruption
Like bullets piercing walls
Creating havoc at city halls
Devising plans
Numerous as the sand
Advising leaders
To elevate teachers
My pen is a sword.

No sleep, no slumber
Will not falter
Despised, even rejected
Will not be intimidated
Weathering the storms
By raising alarms
A friend of the poor
Seeking a cure
Pressuring chiefs
Exacting relief
My pen is a sword.

Like a blazing fire
Will not be extinguished
Motivated by the truth
Will not compromise
Cuts like a knife
Accepts no bribe
The undiluted fury
Judge and jury
A true warrior
Braving danger
My pen is a sword.

Wayward to alignment
Misses no assignment
A friend of the needy
Damning the greedy
Creating diversions
While seeking solutions
Tender and caring

Always sharing
Guardian to the orphans
Husband to the widows
My pen is a sword.

Fair and honest
Will not be prejudiced
Exposing segregation
Facing confrontation
Down in the trenches
Or on court benches
Sitting in the pew
Taking a cue
Constructive criticism
Investigative journalism
Prone to mistakes
Bearing no hate
My pen is a sword.

RASTA

JAH is a lamp unto my feet
A light unto my path
Protector of my life
Defender of my rights...
JAH is GOD
Christ is the son of JAH
Ras Tafari is Christ
In His kingly character
His Imperial Majesty
Emperor Haile Sellassie I of Ethiopia
King of Kings
Lord of Lords
Conquering Lion of Judah
Elect of God
And Light of the world
Son of Israel's King Solomon
And Sheba's Queen Makeda

Rasta is Godly
Rasta is natural
Rasta is creative
Rasta is loving
Rasta is unifying
Rasta is humble
Rasta holds fast to the truth
Rasta guides the youth

Rasta promotes justice
Rasta bears no malice
Rasta advocates equality
Rasta defends humanity

Rasta waves the red gold and green
Rasta protects and provides for his queen
Rasta's symbol is the Lion
Rasta lives upon Mount Zion

Marcus Garvey ignited the passion
Locks and discipline set the fashion
Jamaicans set the pace
To uplift the human race
Rastafarian's greatest desire
Is to return to Mother Africa
Rasta is a beacon to all nations
Get with the revolution.

START

It's a new day
A new dawn
A new beginning
A little bird chirps
New grass sprouts
A flower blooms
With fragrance of perfume
Fresh water springs
From the earth within
As the morning dew burns away
The sunlight brightens another day.

FINDING YOURSELF

Take a stroll into the woods
Deep into the woods
Where listening is learning
Then listen to the wind
As it moves through the trees
Listen to the rustling of the leaves
As they brush against each other
Watch as grass blades bend in unison
This way then that
Listen to the sound
Of your own breathing
Your heart beating
The birds singing
No you are not alone
You are like the wind
The trees
The grass
The birds
You're in harmony
With creation
In a totally natural world
Conversing with your soul
Finding yourself
Being yourself
At peace with yourself
If you can't be yourself

HUTCHIE SIMEON, RAS TAMBA

You are nobody.

THE SOLUTION

Only education
Can remedy our problems
Teach the youth the truth
Teach them the importance of learning
That will determine their future earnings
Let them know a positive attitude
Will see them through

Only education
Will uplift a nation
Teach the youth the truth
Educate them to be productive citizens
So they won't end up in prison
Teach them to be model students
And they will be prudent

Only education
Will solve gang banging
Teach the youth the truth
Give them a solid foundation
And many won't be on probation
Let them know life is no fantasy
Suffering and starvation are realities

Only education
Can conquer deprivation

Teach the youth the truth
Teach them self esteem
So they can fulfill their dreams
Let them know there is a way
But in school they'll have to stay

Only education
Can reverse a bad situation
Teach the youth the truth
Educate them to respect teachers
So they too may become teachers
Let them know education is the tool
If they want to be cool.

AWARENESS

Knowing where
You are coming from
Is important
In knowing where
You are going
For if you don't know
From whence you came
You may not realize
Your goal
When you get there.

MOTHER OF CREATION

Many times you cried
She wiped your eyes
When you were sick
She did not quit
She nourished and cherished
Wiped your nose
And doctored you
Isn't she special
Don't call her a bitch
She is woman
Mother of creation

With her charm
She kept you warm
On the coldest winter night
She held you tight
She is female
Ideal companion of man
She does the chores
Makes it comfortable indoors
Isn't that sweet
Don't call her a bitch
She is woman
Mother of civilization

With her lips on your lips
Sometimes dreaming of her kiss
She is your lover
And a partner a soul mate
Your wife and best friend
The mother of your children
Isn't that nice
Don't call her a bitch
She is woman
Mother of all nations.

A SISTER

The beauty of a sister
Not her outward appearance
Not just her friendly face
Or her moist thick lips
The beauty of a sister
Is her mind, her soul

The beauty of a sister
Sparkles in her eyes
In her soothing voice
Not the bulge of her hips
The beauty of a sister
Lingers in her touch

The beauty of a sister
Is being articulate and independent
Caring and sharing
Teaching and nurturing
The beauty of a sister
Is loving and giving

The beauty of a sister
Not her complexion
Or being a sex symbol
Nor her unique figure

The beauty of a sister
Is motherhood and kindness

The beauty of a sister
Not her apparel
Or her flouncing walk
But her motivation to excel
The beauty of a sister
Is strength to a brother

BLACK WOMAN

The dark brown shade
Of your velvet skin
Touches so deep
To the soul within
Your radiance glows
While your charm
Gives one the shivers
And makes heads spin

The piercing stare
Of your ebony eyes
Burns like fire
And triggers one's desire
The shining ray
Of your beauty
Makes mouths sag
And hearts skip beats

All nations lust
Your protruding bust
The thick full lips
Your round firm hips
Strong in feature
Outstanding figure
The very example
Of female perfection

A tower of strength
Your duty never ends
Mother of all nations
The envy of all races
Energized by vision
Giver of affection
Sharing your love
Like a blessing from above.

BLACK PEARL

Climbed over Mount Everest
Roamed the peaks of
The Rocky Mountains
Swam the raging Amazon
Forged the tempest of the Pacific
Trod endless plains and valleys
Braved the wicked Sahara
Touched all seven continents
Even saw hopping Kangaroos
In the Outback down under
All in search of a single pearl

Looking for one single stalk
Lost in a world of hay fields
Having not the slightest
Inclination of statistics
Or demographics
Concerning this precious jewel
Yet one wandered energized
Only by visions and expectations
Like a straggler lost in the pursuit
Of this black pearl

Zigzagging through cities
Down winding trails

Narrow lanes
Across busy streets
Into cul-de-sacs
Highways and byways
Over mine fields
Along life's dusty roads
All one's life caught up
In this great adventure
Driven only by will
And determination
To fill a void

Such quests must have been made
By mankind all through the ages
Sometimes one would wonder
Is it fantasy
But would maintain it is reality
As it is written take unto thyself
A woman and make her your wife
This soul is waiting
A jewel so precious
Cannot stay undiscovered
Forever

This soul has walked uprightly
Did mostly what was expected
Yet lacks the fulfillment
A feeling of tranquility
Of completeness
With self and the other

Half of the equation
A priceless gem
More precious than all metals
Is this black pearl.

A POSITIVE PLAN

Years will pass
The Negro race will last
But will have paid the cost
For without a positive plan
Victimization and oppression
Will overcome the black man
As only the educated mind
Will overcome hard times
Nigger is stagnant
So they will be erased
The Negro will grow
Because education
Will save us in depression

Rich in talent
And material skills
Yet poor in will
And the ability to build
No hope for the black man
Without education
And a positive plan.

A TRUE DISCIPLE

A brother is a title
Given to a true disciple
An outstanding leader
And a supportive father
He commands respect
In every aspect

A brother is a sample
Sets a good example
Excelling is his only ambition
He is security and protection
A model husband
And a devoted family man

A brother is a mentor
Strong but admits his wrongs
He is a natural provider
Not a divider
He complements
And is complemented

A brother is no gangster
He is a soldier
Making calculated decisions
Always with good intentions

He administers justice
And is not prejudiced

A brother is disciplined
Compassionate and caring
A humanitarian
Adjusts to any situation
He is not complacent
Always accepts a challenge

A brother is a role model
Has no time to idle
Refrains from being a victim
Instead he uses the system
He always sets a high standard
And strives to attain his goals.

ECHOES OF MUSIC

Tis the sound of music
That sounds so sweet and clear
That sweet enchanting music
Blowing through the air
Brings back cherished memories
Of events over the years

Tis the sound of music
Coming from the fair
That vibrating music
Climbing every stair
You need no invitation
Just join in if you care

Tis the sound of music
And dancing in the park
That soft romantic music
A spotlight in the dark
Entertaining and relaxing
Solace for heavy hearts

Tis the sound of music
At a party on the beach
That harmonious music
All within your reach

You can't resist the feeling
Go have yourself a treat

Tis the sound of music
Of flutes and strings and drums
That soul searching music
Bidding all to come
So join the festive gathering
With revelers having fun.

A FRIEND

If a brother is a brother
Then who is a friend?

Give me my brethren
Keep your friend
And all other fiends
You keep them
Fiends are only
Friends
When in need.

MAROONED

Living in Rome
Longing to go home
Grabbed a flight
Joyous and hyped
Smooth landing
Feeling privileged
Then comes the burn
When trying to return

Making the run
Your only concern
But you need documents
From the government
You're backed against the wall
. Dealing with city hall
Marooned on an island
Full of corruption

With papers lost
You're put to the task
Seeking connections
Is a normal reaction
Someone who knows something
Can pull a string
But all connections fail
Your efforts to no avail

To keep hope alive
You're exposed to bribe
With no cash
You're treated like trash
Now you're a victim
Of a corrupt system
Nothing but confusion
When cheated and abandoned

You don't have to cry
If you can buy
Greasing a palm
Is just the norm
A phone call from Mr. Brown
Can turn things around
Anything is possible
In Third World countries.

LONESOME

All alone without a home
Hungry with no money
Friends are no neighbors
Money your only friend
Laugh when you're sad
Curse when you're mad
Everything's a fake
You are asleep
Couldn't be awake

It's lonesome here
Companion a bottle of beer
One job can't pay the bills
Without college skills
Backed in a corner
Watching the rich and greedy
Zooming by
Shunning the poor and needy
Here everyone's an enemy
In the city there's no pity.

POVERTY

If I could find the cure
For being poor
Then life wouldn't
Be such a bore
Without a big paycheck
You have to live and fret
And then some take steps
Come into your life
Bringing more strife
Boost up your mind
Build up your courage
Then drop you like
A dirty towel
Saying your mind
Is in the gutter
Because their bread is buttered
They can't see
That you suffer

If I could find the cure
For poverty
I would live
On a large property
But the paycheck is meager
You always have to borrow
Living from hand to mouth

Your life story spread
All about
And because things
Are not right
You stay up all night
Trying to decipher
Life's mysteries
Forgetting your pride
And sacrificing
Your dignity.

TRY HUMANITY

Don't put your trust in vanity
Try humanity
Food is not short
But the rich got no heart
Greedily you close the door
Without compassion
For the poor

Don't put your trust in vanity
Try humanity
Give him supper
Even bread without butter
Invest more capital
And stop being anti-social

Let us come together
And build one shelter.

WELCOME MANDELA

Greetings Mandela, Welcome my brother!
Long time now man and man a suffer
Denying human rights and United Nations
They held you captive
To subdue your motive

Greetings Mandela, Welcome my brother!
Long time now man and man a utter
Without regard for humanity
Or respect for God Almighty
You were denied your privilege
By a minority acting primitive

Greetings Mandela, Welcome my brother!
Long time now man and man get scattered
Besieging heads of government
And members of Parliament
Who shunned you in bondage
Still you shone like a beacon

Greetings Mandela, Welcome my brother!
Long time now the battle getting hotter
With respect to all supporters
And all the slain brothers
We welcome you to our territory
A true stalwart of Africa.

MANDELA VICTOROUS

Come come come Mandela
Come come rise to power
You struggled not in vain
Victory you have gained
Now you come to reign
Come come come Mandela
Come come rule South Africa

Come come come Mandela
Come come rise to power
From the dungeon of Pretoria
God has answered your prayer
Set the whole world on fire
Even cause Botha to retire
Come come come Mandela
Come come rule South Africa

Come come come Mandela
Come come rise to power
You've got the vision
DeClerk has made his decision
Tear down the bars of iron
Now you walk a free man
Come come come Mandela
Come come rule South Africa.

FOUNDATION

To function as one people
Black people
Must be willing to support
Their own industry and commerce
Help a brother in need
Make it easier for him to lead.

To function as a team
Black people
Must wake up to reality
Establish their identity
Practice unity among one another
And give respect to each other.

To function with one destiny
Black people
Must practice their own version of religion
To ward off intrusion
Fight against encroachment
But welcome development.

To function as one unit
Black people
Must develop a united foreign policy
Defend African unity

Overcome starvation
By removing stagnation.

To function with one love
Black people
Must be grateful of the privilege
To protect their heritage
Be militant and aggressive
To weed out all liabilities.

To function as a nation
Black people
Must show their ability
Stand up for integrity
Encourage and utilize production
The foundation of a strong nation.

SWORD

ATROCITY

It's hard to digest
Unresolved and unredressed
It is fact not fiction
The rampant abduction
And capture of Africans
A unanimous decision
Of Europeans
To sell Africans
On western plantations

Our past is worse
Than any holocaust
Imagine the hell it caused
The weeping destitute families
Chained and bound
Crammed like sardines in a tin
Aboard a ship of doom
Across the Atlantic stretch
Steered by the devil's advocates

The brutal injustice
The carnage the atrocity
The inhumane oppression
Upon unfortunate Africans
Mother Africa howled
Bound her belly and bawled

HUTCHIE SIMEON, RAS TAMBA

Spine crushed dignity raped
Millions of her children
Like sheep
On the auction block
Bare feet bare backs

They languished in pain
Their cries were in vain
While the barbarians raved
To satisfy their gluttonous crave
Greed filled their eyes
They couldn't hear the cries
Of their human cargo
In the maw of the slaver's ship

They murdered our brothers
Raped our sisters
The whip in their hands
Made scars on their backs
Whenever it clapped
Like an electric shock
It sent shivers up their spines
Many lay bleeding, some dying
Bearing the heat of summer
Braving the chill of winter
It didn't matter

Filthy and raggedy
Half naked and bare feet
I can still hear my sisters weep
See my brothers bleed

While their children plead
And every time the whip clapped
A sudden heart attack

That atrocity
Was not only on the Black Man
It was on humanity.

SLAVERY DAYS

Because we were not white
They thought we were not polite
Because we were black
They made us stay at the back
But when we spoke our language
They were astonished
We showed them gold
And lust filled their souls

Because we were not white
They treated us with spite
Because we were black
They put us into barracks
Then they ravished our women
And humiliated our men
Let us feel like lions in a den

Because we were not white
They robbed our birthrights
Because we were black
We carried sacks on our backs
When we sowed the wheat
They reaped the sweets
They drove in buggies
While we walked on bare feet.

THE WHIP

Lord! When mi member
The whip
Every time mi member
Mi blood run cold
It retrieves memories of
Piracy and slavery
Shackles on our feet
Heavy chains around our neck
No shirt on our backs
Piece of cloth round our waist
Sheltered by the mercy
Of the red hot sun
Then the whip
Every time it clapped
It caused a shock
One more clap
And one brother dropped
On his knees
Blood running down his back
Lord! When mi member
The whip

Every time mi member
Mi blood run cold
Sisters and brothers
Chained together

Pregnant women
Mothers with babies
Strapped to their backs
Backra on his horse
Under a big broad hat
Armed with a gun
And a big long whip
Every time it clapped
It caused a shock
One more clap
And sister dropped
Yet another clap
And a premature baby
Was born on the spot
Lord! When mi member
The whip

Every time mi member
Mi blood run cold
Blackman strapped
Over barrel naked
Ten lashes from
The cat-o-nine
One of the penalties
In colonial time
Some pee some d____
How can they call us lazy
That's why I call them crazy
They don't remember slavery
And how many lives it cost
In South Africa Rhodesia

Sudan Mogadishu
On the plantations
Lord! When mi member
The whip

Every time mi member
Mi blood run cold
Taken off the chain
Given cocaine
That white rock
Makes men wear frocks
Drugged dead or detained
That is the plan
For today's black man
Lord! When mi member
The whip.

500 YEARS

500 years is a long time
What is your plan
I don't understand
500 years is a long time
What is your plan
For the black man
We want to return
To the motherland
500 years in Rome
It's time to go home
Tired of your system
Your bad upbringing
500 years is a long time
Tired of scrubbing your floors
And tilling your soil
While you keep the spoils
Yes master, yes sir boss
Won't work no more
Cause we will not bow
Or lift our crown
To expose our dreads
500 years is a long, long time
We need a pension
And full redemption.

NOT YET PAID

For work done
In the cotton fields
Of Alabama
We have not been paid

The tobacco fields
Of Virginia
We have not been paid

The sugar cane plantations
Of the Caribbean
We have not been paid

And all other plantations
In the western hemisphere
We have not been paid

It's almost time
To take my rest
So let me know
When it's time to collect.

BETRAYAL

They betrayed our trust
They were only desirous
Of satisfying their lust
We received them with open arms
Opened our doors
And let them into our souls
They repaid our kindness
With brutal injustice
Selling us into slavery
By deception and trickery
To be freed of this conspiracy
Is to achieve mental victory.

A BLACK MAN WONDERS

I wonder
What we did to suffer so
It worries my brain
How they released the chain
But still have the cane
Inflicting grief and pain
They raped Mother Africa
Of her sons and daughters
Robbed her of gold
Diamond and silver
Denied her culture
And treated her as inferior

I wonder
What we did to suffer so
They came at random
Stole our freedom
Told us to watch and pray
Till Jesus come
With milk and honey
And paradise plum
That could fool only some

I wonder
What we did to suffer so
Some came with the Bible

Claimed to be Jah's disciples
Wearing a cross
Claiming to be men of the cloth
But they looked more like coots
In knee-high boots
Granting emancipation
Without restitution
Denying freedom of religion
And a proper education
Targeting us for humiliation

I wonder
What we did to suffer so
Some claim population explosion
Led to the invention of pills and condoms
But their plan was to restrict
The Black Man
To make him a minority
In his own homeland
That did not work
So they invented AIDS
Sending millions to the grave

I wonder
What we did to suffer so
Because they live in fantasy
Seeking wealth and prosperity
To lengthen their life expectancy
While our tribulations and trials
Cause some to bow to Baal

And some to worship other idols
While others put their trust in vials
And disturb the dead after burial.

BELLS OF FREEDOM

The world is changing
The walls of segregation
Are crumbling
The reign of terror
Will soon be over
Now bells of freedom
Are ringing all over
Let there be justice
In Africa now.

BONDAGE

Coming here
Were no volunteers
Sold into bondage
Shipped to the west
Traveling for days
Weeks and months
The wicked tempests
Disease and insects
Sailing on and on
Chained and bound
Stripped and whipped
Deprived of our identity
Culture and language
Feeble thrown overboard
While great big bucks
Fetched a high price
On the auction blocks
Branded like animals
Fed like vultures
Working night and day
While the bosses
Kept our pay
Hurt and starving
We slaved
To complain meant the whip

HUTCHIE SIMEON, RAS TAMBA

Tar and feather
Stake or tree
They showed no mercy.

RUMORS

Every day them a chat
About this about that
But only they alone can chat
Marcus Garvey was framed
Martin Luther King
Never survived the attack

Delegates and Heads of States
Have authority to chat
That privilege poor people lack
Mahatma Ghandi suffered
Malcolm X too
Was gunned down on the spot

Personalities on TV
Get paid to chat
Not riff-raff or small sprats
Tianamen Square wasn't prepared
Ghadaffi bragged
Till Reagan rushed him and licked shots

Attorneys and magistrates
Have profession to chat
Minorities are suspects that's a fact
Nelson Mandela poor fellow

HUTCHIE SIMEON, RAS TAMBA

Christ was crucified
And paid the price for that

Millionaires and celebrities
Let them chat
Poor people please stay back
Natty Dread
Or any other nappy heads
Don't you ever try that.

ORGANIZE

It's time to organize
Forget false pride
And get centralized
Because people without culture
Are worse than vultures

It's time to recognize
The power of our history
Though marred by slavery
Still our inventions
Are the greatest since Creation

Leave the other man's factories
Stop dreaming of fantasies
And start our own industries
Because people without a future
Are like dry bones in a sepulcher

They will hire you
Don't like you they will fire you
Or work you then retire you
So what is your intention
To strengthen the other man's religion

They will laugh with you
And talk with you

Turn around and slaughter you
Because a people in captivity
Are a people without power

The black man's redemption
Is to reclaim the Motherland
And evict all tenants
Because people without roots
Are like parasites that lost their bite.

AWAKE

Mind poisoned
Vision obscured
You are living a dream
Come awake black nation
Up from your slumber
This is a real world
Where good and bad
Walk hand in hand
Where poverty exists
As do riches
Where robbers
Roam the streets
Searching for prey
A salesman
A lawyer
A doctor
A preacher
A politician
In any form
Or fashion
Stay awake
Black nation
Stay awake.

DISCRIMINATION

Every day blam the door slams
Against another black man
Convict is the verdict
But who is the culprit
They commit the crime
We serve the time
Locked up in jail without bail
For days months years
That's not right
Them things make me sick!

Born into a system
Where color makes you a victim
With no natural inclination
Towards crime nor violence
A citizen of the ghettos
Where honest workers regress
And cons and dons progress
So it's we they call thugs
But who invented drugs
Twisted, isn't it
Them things make me sick!

Every day brag-a dap
Another brother drops
Not from a heart attack

But a policeman's gun shot
Victim of the system
Racial profiling
Against black people
Police brutality
Against minorities
Now face the reality
There will be no equality
While they have authority
Them things make me sick!

Every day in the hood
It's rat-a-tat-tat
Gangsters firing shots
Brothers killing brothers
It's not coincidental
It's intentional
Killing your own was never a concern
It's planned and it makes some richer
Like lawyers doctors
Judges and executioners
Even the gun manufacturers
Can't you see
Them things make me sick!

Communist socialist or democratic
It's the same folly tricks
Designed to suppress
Sabotage undermined and infiltrate
All motives to create frustration
Against any creation
That is not their invention

While in this civilization
They grant permission
For one man to marry another man
And legalize lesbians
Isn't that Satan in action
Them things make me sick!

Ozone layer depletion
Nuclear waste pollution
Disease invention
All weapons of mass destruction
For which there is no solution
While hunger and malnutrition
Starvation and homelessness
Caused by poverty
In Third World countries
Leave super powers
To play war games
With stockpiles of nuclear weapons
Them things make me sick!

Every day frustration
Leads to demonstrations
Where opposition
Sometimes turns into rebellion
Cranking up the battalions
To wage war on civilians
Treated without impunity
Granted no immunity
Their justice is our injustice
Selfish, isn't it
Dem things make me sick!

NOT GUILTY

How do you plead
Guilty or not guilty
Asked the judge
Your honor
You are full of bigotry
An accomplice
To the crime
You are malicious
And prejudiced
Administering injustice
I am not guilty
It was self defense
My reflexes got
The better of me
I saw him before
He saw me
And I was blinded
By subordination
Hunger and starvation
Chased by ravenous beasts
Mocked and shot at
Had I been caught
I would have been hanged
Tied to the stake
Or burned alive
Tarred and feathered

The fate of two brothers
While they chained
And dragged to death
Another.

APARTHEID

I and I vex
How they killed Malcolm X
Assassinated Martin Luther King
And crucified Jesus Christ
So tell George Bush
And the one Maggie Thatcher
They can't lift the sanctions
Off South Africa
Till we lick some sense
In the one Botha
And wipe out apartheid
In South Africa

It's a shame
How they gave Marcus Garvey
The blame
A brilliant philosopher
And a great organizer
Let us lick some shots
For Paul Bogle
Lick some shots
For Sister Nanny
Come let us lick some shots
For Sam Sharpe and Cudjoe
And all freedom fighters
Defending Africans

Twenty one gun salute
For Jomo Kenyatta
And his artical brethren
Tom Mboya
And lick some more
For the Mau Mau warriors
For evicting the squatters
And ruling Kenya
Come let us lick some shots
For our brethren Malcolm
Lick nuff shots on Babylon kingdom

Let's lick some shots
For all black heroes
Those from yesterday
And the ones for tomorrow
Lick some shots
For Nelson Mandela
One barrage of shots
For each day spent in prison
Lick some shots
For Martin Luther King
And all the people
Who marched with him

Respect due to
Sister Rosa Parks
Harriet Tubman
And Mohammed Ali
They never bowed
To Babylon's system

Now it's justice for all
Or no peace at all
We will take our freedom
Anyway it comes
No sympathy
For the one DeClerk
It's one hundred percent freedom
Or shots nonstop

Twenty one gun salute
To Winnie Mandela
A militant sister
A true freedom fighter
Take up the Bible
The bullet and the gun
And we won't put it down
Till freedom come
We will march from
Soweto to Pretoria
From Johannesburg to Victoria
Tell George Bush
And tell Maggie Thatcher
No bother lift the sanction
Off South Africa
Till we lick some sense
In the one Botha
And end all apartheid
In South Africa.

UNITY

Organization promotes leaders
Education creates builders
Unity brings brothers
And sisters flocking together
Building one big shelter
Because a loner is a goner
A wolf without a pack
A sheep without a flock
A lamb to the slaughter
Poised for disaster.

EQUALITY

Take back authority
Give up apartheid
Away with segregation
Up with equality

Give us justice
Remove state of emergency
Away with oppression
Up with solidarity

Give us respect
Back off victimization
Away with racism
Up with reality.

COWBOY JUSTICE

War is not the answer
It causes too much hate
For the people of the United States
Is it by choice
We are paying the price
Living in hell
Thinking it swell
Afraid to expose our nationality
In every foreign country
Fearing hostility
For the government's foreign policy

This is a nation
With a reputation
For human rights violation
Destabilizing poor nations
Sabotages and sanctions
Triggering adverse reactions
Of suffering and starvation
But no-one dares
To levy citations
In awe of military might
Should it come to a fight

MY PEN IS A SWORD

Nations live in fear
Some downright scared
Of your veto power
And being the superpower
With weapons of mass destruction
Tainted by corruption
Demonstrating cowboy justice
And ramrod politics

This nation is living in darkness
Lacking insight into our policies
New Orleans had no priority
Still no official apology
For the lack of urgency
By FEMA and other agencies
Resulting in death and destruction
Which leads us to the question
How can one be a refugee
In one's own country?

Who would have believed
This could happen here?
Only in places like Africa
Asia or Central America
This is a huge disgrace
On the great United States
People still wait in limbo
While authorities look bewildered

Could this be ethnic cleansing
The levy breaching?

YOU'RE FULL OF IT

I ain't gonna take
Your (----) no more
You'll have to come better
And that's for sure
You hate my guts
Because I'm poor
Don't expect an apology
That's my analogy
So I ain't gonna take
Your(----) no more
You despised my being
But my hands are clean
Don't even try
You know you lied
And don't call me that
I'm not your friend
Cause I ain't gonna take
Your(----)no more
Practice what you preach
You blasted thief
And if I cuss
Your words I don't trust
Don't expect pity
With those crocodile tears
And I ain't gonna take
Your(----)no more

Pack your things
And hit the door
You have your say
And had your day
What you said
You did not do
And what you did
I have no clue
So I ain't gonna take
Your(----)no more
You haven't a cure
And I have a sore.

STOP THE CRIME

A full time
Dem stop the crime
No carry go
Just bring it come
We want our freedom now
We negotiate
Participate
And even demonstrate
But nothing alleviates
The situation
In Africa

Free election in Poland
Downed the wall
Of separation in Germany
Making Baltic independent states
And welcomed the Kremlin
To western discipline
Denounced military aggression
In Tiananmen Square
Lick shot on Iraq
To evict Saddham
Out of Kuwait
How much longer must
The Africans wait?

A full time
Dem stop the crime!

ATTENTION UNITED NATIONS

Attention United Nations
You have a record
Of upholding discrimination
Against developing nations

Their systems of justice
Are prejudiced
Judges and juries are racist
Always upholding culprits
Who frame colored people
As bandits

Hurting
From the days of slavery
No recompense through democracy
All oppositions sent to prison
Apartheid is one example
Of injustice and humiliation
Upheld by the United Nations

Nelson Mandela
Got no compensation
His release is little consolation
For no intervention
Regarding the rights
Of the black man

Those in authority are criminals
Upholding thugs and gangsters
Choosing not to educate youngsters
Preferring to eradicate all militants
Who dare to challenge their decisions

We know about their history
And their barbarous activities
Like slavery lies and trickery
Sons and daughters of pirates
Mothers and fathers of hypocrites
Educating thieves to preach on pulpits

We know about the lynching
Of poor defenseless victims
What could have provoked
The burnings
Of less fortunate brethren

Attention United Nations
You have a record
Of upholding discrimination
Against developing nations
Make amends
For the injustice
For the bloody reward
You inherited

MY PEN IS A SWORD

Their dynasties are of the devil
Their deeds and actions are evil
Revoke their laws of tyranny
That make our people targets
It's time to show some sympathy
And stop the AIDS catastrophe

If there's a Hell they are destined
If there's a Heaven they are forbidden
For the crime of murder they are guilty
Destabilizing governments is their policy
It's time to stop the atrocity
Let there be peace and prosperity

We know of their lust for vanity
And their involvement in bribery
Their constitutions have no integrity
They fill life with misery
For people they deem as minority

They still make heroes of criminals
Sending pirates as ambassadors
Their kingdoms founded on corruption
Are bound to fall as Babylon.

DON'T MESS WITH AFRICA

Down in Pretoria
They ruled by apartheid
Up in Ethiopia
They fought against Jahovah
Brothers against brothers
Even sisters turned warriors
Defending a political objective
Not invented by the natives

Over in Sudan
They fought the Armageddon
Forces of religious dictators
Disorienting poor settlers
Causing death and starvation
Separation and mass migration

Down in Rhodesia
Smith waged racial segregation
Up with Zimbabwe
And stop foreign intrusion

Over in Kenya
Under British domination
Kenyatta and the Mau Mau warriors
Fought and overcame discrimination

Once in Uganda
Idi Amin made us wonder
Driving the colonialist band
From his forefathers' land

After Mussolini
Invaded the Ethiopians
His fascists were ejected
From the Motherland

Across the desert straits
Into Kuwait
Bands of Americans
Locked horns with Saddham
Greedy for power
Death before dishonor
It's blood and oil
And dead bodies for miles

Watch the Palestinians
Deprived of a homeland
While the leaders of Israel
Arabs call them infidels
Captured the West Bank
And rule with armored tanks
Yet with all the hostage taking
They still have America's backing

Check out Liberia
Deadlocked for power
Shall freedom come
In this new hour?

HUTCHIE SIMEON, RAS TAMBA

Black Hawk down in Somalia
Apartheid crushed in South Africa
Fascists ousted from Ethiopia
Don't mess with Africa!

SERIOUS

Dem couldn't be serious
Cow jump over the moon
Dish run away with the spoon
And how mankind comes
From baboon
That is why I am shy
Of their injections
Cause you really don't know
Their intentions.

PROTECTION

Protection Jah Protection
Be our defense against
Oppression
It's his credit card
His Scotland Yard
He is the inventor
Of all the fraud
Give us some respect
For our inventions
Africa is the mother
Of all civilization

Protection Jah protection
Be our defense against
Infiltration
It's his CIA
It's his KGB
He rules the land
The air and sea
We are not for war
Yet we carry the scars
We are not inferior
But his weapons
Are superior

Protection Jah protection
Be our defense against
Domination
They issue visas
They control the media
And they dictate to
United Nations
And what is shown
On television
They even disarmed
Our warriors
And turned some into
AIDS carriers

Protection Jah Protection
Be our assurance against
The evil ones
They hold the handle
We hold the blade
They cause the hurt
And deny us first aid
We brave the storm
Toiling on the farm
Gathering the hay
Yet they have the say

Protection Jah Protection
Be our defense against
The other man
He has the gun
He has the bomb
He makes the law

HUTCHIE SIMEON, RAS TAMBA

Governing all nations
So what's the intention
Of all those missile inventions
And where is the solution
For disease infestations?

HOMELESS

When it rains
It causes me grief
I should be thankful
For the blessing
But I curse the rain
Cause I don't have a house
I am the raggedy person
Who sleeps under the bridge

I hate winter oh so cruel
Snow could be fun
All white and crunchy
Yet I yearn for summer days
Cause I live outdoors
I'm the child
You pass at the corner
Shivering in the cold

You won't believe this
I hate summer too
It is unbearable heat
Sweaty, sticky and uncomfortable
Shower is a luxury I can't afford
I'm the one
You hate to see everyday
As you drive by

Christmas is a time for the rich
Not for me
The have not
I detest such occasions
Why should I be happy
When deprived and forgotten
I'm he with the Santa Claus hat
I clean windshields for a tip

In sickness I curse doctors
There is no denying
They can cure some illnesses
 But why should I give credit
To a profession
I do not inherit
I'm the beggar at the traffic light
You rolled up your windows to ignore

I cry for hunger
But shed no tears
Yes my stomach growls
It hurts to the very core
But you'll see no tears in my eyes
Yet I am flooded inside
I'm the old bag woman
Pushing the shopping cart.

ROBBED

Laborer gets robbed
Boss man keeps the bag
Working AM thru PM
But dollars don't make sense
So labor for hire
Until you retire
Sometimes pay gets cut
While cost-of-living
Steadily goes up.

CONFUSION

Love is lovely
War is ugly
Soul searching
Nuclear disarming
Brothers against brothers

Gays and lesbians
Fighting for equality
Demanding from society
Good golly

Rich getting richer
Poor getting poorer
No end to violence
Who are the victims

Underprivileged
Children
No place to play
Searching rubbish heaps
Looking for food to eat
No toy for the have nots
While dogs sporting platinum
Ride in prams...

A THOUGHT

The farmers sow
The reapers reap
Careful what you sow
Cause that you shall reap
When the harvest is bright
It brings delight
Without the rain
They plow in vain.

STATE OF EMERGENCY

In a state of emergency
Police nuh use dem intelligency
Dem always inna urgency
Thats how they kill all the likkle baby

In a state of emergency
Dem use political strategy
Through governmental bureaucracy
Fi wipe out opposition to dem policy

In a state of emergency
When dem tun off the electricity
Merciful Jah, show some pity
Or gunman woulda kill off everybody

In a state of emergency
Authority use nuff diplomacy
Without regard for humanity
Dem kill off poor people pickinny

In a state of emergency
When all o' Satan's disciples
Wid sixteen and repeater rifles
Terrorize even di baby pon di nipple

MY PEN IS A SWORD

In a state of emergency
Dem give police di authority
Fi beat an detain anybody
Who nuh come from di upper society

In a state of emergency
A pure confusion inna di city
Police inna helmit carrying baton
Curfew di whole a di community

In a state of emergency
Police mistreat ghetto citizen
Dem nuh use dem ability
Pure brute force an ignorancy.

INVASION

Attack Iraq capture Saddam
Now it's time for Iran
And then the North Koreans
Try to subdue all nations
Acquiring nuclear weapons
Only mister white
Will be considered alright

Why can't Third World countries
Acquire nuclear technology
Is it your intention
That such an invention
Belongs only to one man
So you put them in line
Or whip their behinds

When will it stop
The war in Iraq
Too many of our troops
Coming back in sacks
End the invasion now
Bring the troops back
And stop the attack

Bring the troops back
We didn't have to attack
Admit we were wrong
No need to stick to the plan
Be a man we'll understand
Bring them back
Too many body bags coming back

Bring them back
Duty we did not lack
Come home today
Don't wait for tomorrow
Or we'll create another Sahara
So much pain
What is the gain

What is victory
Is it fame or pride
Or is it making history?

WHY

Why oh why
Should it make you happy
When children cry
Why should it make you sad
To see others glad
Oh what folly
The things that make you jolly
Is there blood in your veins
Or water from the rain
It is someone's friend
Or a neighbor's daughter
The other man's son
That suffers the pain
Why oh why
Does it make you pleased
To see others bleed
Why should it cause you sorrow
At a pleasant tomorrow?

GIMME A BREAK

Gimme a break
I slept late
Never letf my gate
I was in bed all the time
Couldn't have committed the crime
Shivering with fear
I was scared
Now indefinite detention
No court date mentioned
I tried to flee
They wrestled me to my knees
I begged I pleaded
No one heeded
An innocent man
In a den of scorpions
Confusion in the dungeon
Sleepless nights
The constant fights
Not even a pillow
Under my head
Not a sheet not a spread
The cold concrete for a bed
Cries of pain
The mental strain
Total agony
Men dwelling in sodomy

The seasoned are chronic
While the weak panic
It is pure hell
Not a place to dwell
So we demonstrate
Things escalate
It got hot
Warden fired shots
Then it got quiet
But was labeled a riot
One dead
Seven counting lead
What was gained
More restraint
Wanted to make a difference
A positive contribution
Given restitution.

CHAOS

Cannot face another day
Without a job
Nothing to eat
Wife and children to feed
Not even a cent
To pay the rent
Without a ride
You have to hike
Roaming the streets
In search of grub
Weary tired
Endless days
Restless nights
What a plight
Lord mi mumma
Hang down her head
Too proud to beg
Ends can't meet
See the homeless
On the streets
She cried
Tears in her eyes
Can't go on much longer
Crime getting bolder
Hate
Date rape

Remove the slate
Given books
Graduating crooks
Computer age
Some a gaze
Walking in a daze
Phony physicians
Can't trust anyone
Con artists
Next door neighbor
Child molester
Lord mi mumma
Hang down her head
It dread
Her husband dead
Can't buy bread
Children won't be fed
Terrorists and gangsters
All youngsters
Crime
They are willing
Sex
Everyone selling
Go on
Don't stop
That is a man
Wearing a frock
Pure crap
When will it stop
Lord mi mumma
It's rough
Dutty tough

Crime out of control
It's not pretty
In the city
Politicians greedy
No help for the needy
Weeping
Wailing
Gnashing of teeth
Even the dogs
On the street
No respect
People fret
Just looking at a gangster
Could mean instant death
Can't trust anyone
Insurance scam
Lord mi mumma
Hang down her head
She bawl
Headache
Stomach weak
Knees tremble
Lament
Torment
No consideration
For the younger generation
Lord mi mumma
Can't make sense
Out of nonsense
Everything must come to an end...